This Is the Stable

CYNTHIA COTTEN

illustrated by DELANA BETTOLI

Henry Holt and Company ✦ New York

This is the stable, dusty and brown,
in a quiet corner of Bethlehem town.

This is the star whose light shone down

on the quiet stable, dusty and brown.

This is the manger, filled with hay
to feed the animals sheltered away

from the chilly night when the star shone down
on the quiet stable, dusty and brown.

This is the cow with a swishing tail,
whose gentle moo hushed a baby's wail.

This is the donkey, gray and white,
who stood near the manger all through the night.

They both kept watch while the star shone down
on the quiet stable, dusty and brown.

This is the mother, her manner so mild,
singing and rocking her newborn child.

This is her husband, patient and wise,
guarding his family with watchful eyes.

Together they settled the little one down

in the quiet stable, dusty and brown.

These are the shepherds, tending their sheep,

out in the fields while the town was asleep.

These are the angels, a glorious throng,
who sang to the shepherds a wonderful song:

"Be not afraid—go to Bethlehem town,
to the quiet stable, dusty and brown."

These are the wise men, travelers three,
who knew of an ancient prophecy.

They followed the star whose light shone down
on the quiet stable, dusty and brown.

These are their gifts, so fine to behold—
frankincense, myrrh, and glistening gold.

They carried these presents uphill and down
till they reached the stable, dusty and brown.

This is the baby, born that night
in the stable marked by the star so bright.

A baby boy, who cooed and cried
and looked around with eyes so wide.

Then, cuddled and swaddled, he laid his head
on the soft, sweet hay in his manger bed

and slept in the stable in Bethlehem town,
the quiet stable, dusty and brown.

This is the stable, dusty and brown,

in a quiet corner of Bethlehem town.

With the coo of a dove for a lullaby,
the little one slumbered with barely a cry,

safe in the warmth of light and love
while all through the night, in the heavens above,

the angels sang and the star shone down
on the quiet stable in Bethlehem town,
the quiet stable, dusty and brown.

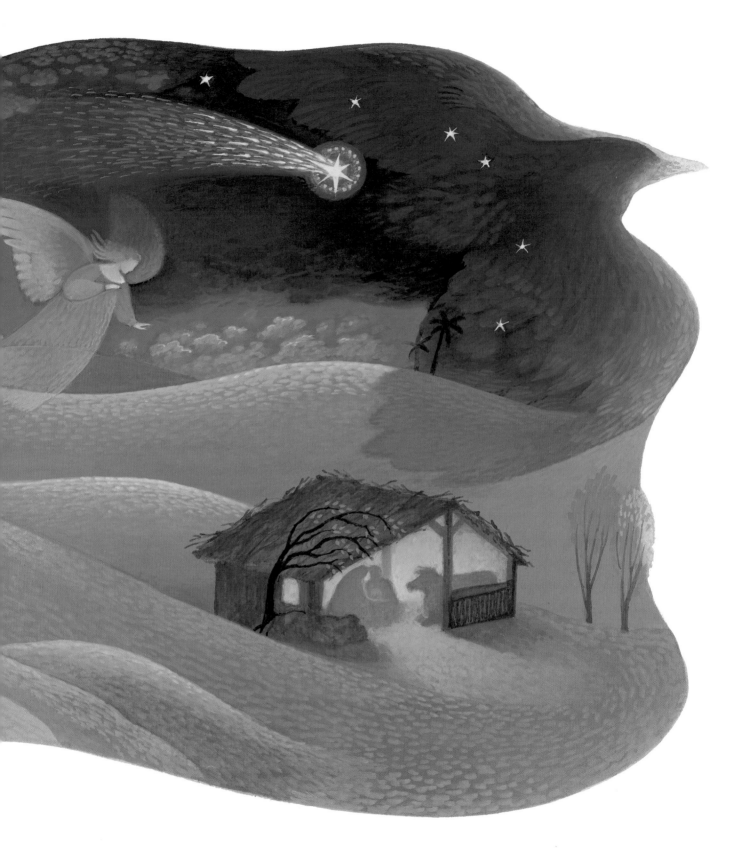

For Pat Easton
and the Monday Night Writers' Group
at the Peters Township Library,
with love and thanks
—C. C.

For my Bethlehem friend Greg . . .
who always believed
—D. B.

Henry Holt and Company, LLC, PUBLISHERS SINCE 1866
175 Fifth Avenue, New York, New York 10010 [www.henryholtchildrensbooks.com]

Henry Holt® is a registered trademark of Henry Holt and Company, LLC.
Text copyright © 2006 by Cynthia Cotten. Illustrations copyright © 2006 by Delana Bettoli.
All rights reserved. Distributed in Canada by H. B. Fenn and Company Ltd.

Library of Congress Cataloging-in-Publication Data
Cotten, Cynthia. This is the stable / Cynthia Cotten; illustrated by Delana Bettoli.—1st ed.   p.   cm.
Summary: Recalls, in rhyming text and illustrations, the Nativity story, from the brown and dusty stable to the star shining brightly above.
ISBN-13: 978-0-8050-7556-4 / ISBN-10: 0-8050-7556-9. 1. Jesus Christ—Nativity—Juvenile fiction. [1. Jesus Christ—Nativity—Fiction. 2. Christmas—
Fiction. 3. Stories in rhyme.] I. Bettoli, Delana, ill. II. Title. PZ8.3.C8284Thi 2006   [E]—dc22   2005019904

First Edition—2006 / Designed by Patrick Collins. The artist used sepia ink outline, watercolor underpainting,
gouache, and acrylic paint to create the illustrations for this book. Printed in Mexico.

3   5   7   9   10   8   6   4   2